THE
POSITIVE
100
APPROACH

AMINA SUAREZ

A MINDFUL APPROACH TO INTENTIONAL MOTHERHOOD

THE
POSITIVE
100
APPROACH

A Mother's Transformation Journey
From Chaos to Calm

To my girls.
You are the inspiration behind everything that I do.
Thank you for shaping me into the mother—and the woman
—I continue to become.
You teach me, every day, what truly matters.

AMINA SUAREZ
Positive 100
A Mum's Transformation Journey From Chaos to Calm

www.positive100.com

This book includes a complimentary reflective
worksheet designed to deepen your awareness and
help you recognise the strengths you already carry.
You'll find access details at the end of the book.

Contents

Introduction

Imagine a morning where your voice is calm, the children are smiling, and there's less yelling echoing through your home. That's the relief I aim to bring with this book, written for the real-world mum just like you.

There are numerous parenting books available, with many voices and varying 'right ways' to do it. But let's be honest, when you're in the thick of parenting, you don't have the time or energy to read a 200-page manual on methods and philosophies. You just want something simple, relatable, and straightforward. That's exactly why I wrote this book.

This isn't about being the perfect parent. It's about being you — the parent who's doing their best, showing up every day, and still feeling like they're running into walls sometimes. This book was created to meet you right where you are.

You'll notice it's split into two parts. The first is a story written for you to see yourself in. It's there to help you slow down, breathe, and step into the shoes of a mum who's probably a lot like you: loving her children deeply but feeling frustrated, tired, and unsure at times. By recognising these shared struggles, you can find comfort in knowing that these feelings are a normal part of life. This normalisation can significantly reduce stress, giving you relief and reassurance that you're not alone.

As you read, keep your awareness open to her mindset — her thoughts, reactions, and the small shifts she begins to make.

Take a moment to reflect: How do you feel when you recognise these struggles? Is it relief knowing you're not alone, hope for change, or curiosity about new strategies? Gently explore these feelings, and let them guide you along the journey of this story.

This first part isn't about change yet. It's about recognition. It's the moment where things begin to make sense — where you start to see yourself, your reactions, and your intentions with more clarity. Simply noticing this is already a shift.

The second part is your action guide. This is where we take what you've seen, felt, and related to in the story, and turn it into something real and practical. The three-part guide isn't about controlling your child, learning something new, or fixing everything overnight. It's about giving shape to what you already know but may not yet have language for. It's an invitation to move with awareness — to notice your patterns, your instincts, and the quiet truth that you already carry as a parent. Rather than telling you who to be or what you must do, this part offers clarity and structure so you can live in alignment with your values, trust your intuition, and parent in a way that feels authentic to you. It's about shifting your mindset—moving from managing your children to mastering yourself. Because when your mindset changes, so does your approach, your peace, and your connection with your children.

You've already taken a powerful step just by picking up this book. That alone says a great deal about your love, your commitment, and your willingness to grow. Your children will benefit from your decision to transform, not through perfection, but through intention. So, take a deep breath. Let this be your gentle reminder that you're doing well — better than you probably give yourself credit for. You don't need to have all the answers; you just need the willingness to see things differently.

And that's what you'll find here — something simple, something relatable, and something real.

I

Part One | When You Start to See It

A space of recognition.
*Through the lens of the mother in this story,
awareness gently unfolds — not as a lesson, but as a
noticing. As you read, pay attention to how she feels,
how she responds, and what becomes clearer simply
by seeing it. Nothing needs to be changed here.
Awareness has already begun.*

The Beginning of the Day

It's 5:28 a.m.

Alarm rings.

You've committed to that extra two minutes to collect your thoughts before opening the quilt. You know you could do with an extra forty minutes of sleep, but if you take it, the kids will be awake before you are.

Yesterday was the day you decided to write a forward action plan, and today you are committed to following it — forever. This plan is all about the new you. The best version of you that is emotionally regulated and radiating grace. You're hopeful that this time, things will work out.

It's now 5:31 a.m. You push the quilt off of you. You step onto the cold floor one foot at a time, and stretch out your back. You hear that satisfying crack. You stand and drag yourself towards the bathroom.

There's a moment of hesitation — whether today is the day. You read in that parenting book you bought last week that the secret to managing your emotions — and helping your children with theirs — starts with the parent getting enough sleep. You understand the importance of sleep because your own emotional capabilities are shaky depending on how much rest you've had. Still, you couldn't help but binge-watch that series on NowTV.

You needed to unwind from the chaos of having to hold it all together, especially after the ordeal at bedtime when Daisy called you mean names for wanting her to brush her teeth. Not to mention you deserve an award for the Olympic sport you participated in last night —getting the kids to sleep before 8:30 p.m.

You take a quick shower and wash off any last bits of bad energy from the past, reminding yourself: today is the new you. You stand for a final moment of pre-day silence— the calm before the storm — and refocus, telling yourself, 'No, I want to manifest positivity from now on. I'm realistic and optimistic. I will be positive and radiate love and calmness, and the kids will just organically follow my lead. I'm in control.'

Off the water goes, then you rush to get yourself dressed. You quickly debate with yourself whether it's a full body lotion day or just the essentials — face, hands, and legs. That would give you five extra minutes to grab a hot drink for the last moments before the team is awake.

You're sipping your coffee whilst leaning on the kitchen surface, your hands hugging the walls of the cup, and you soak in a moment of peace and tranquillity. Then you hear faint footsteps right above you.

It's 6 a.m. on the dot. The first set of little feet is up.

And so... it begins.

But remember, 'this day is different,' you think, shifting your mindset as you finish your coffee. Times have changed: Daisy now gets herself ready for school, brushes her teeth, showers, and dresses herself. It feels like only yesterday you were running her a bath as a baby. Now she's eight and does most things independently.

A rush of pride sets in. Until you hear little feet number two

— Lily, at five — reminding you that independence is still a way off for the younger ones. With baby Jake only six months old, you accept you've got years to go. But a girl can dream, right?

Lily's footsteps, much faster and louder than Daisy's, signal the next transition to a busy morning. You prepare for noise — screams... 'Let's keep it positive,' you remind yourself. As you finish your coffee, you pop some bread in the toaster, ready for the kids to eat once they're done. It's only 6:13 a.m. and with a school departure at half past eight, you're making good time so far.

You hear little voices chatting away. 'How sweet that they're communicating so well together. Oh — wait. Are they talking or arguing right now?'

"Mum!" shouts Daisy.

'Oh, here it goes—the first squabble of the day. What happened now?' You take a deep breath while walking up the stairs, then, as you step onto the landing, you put on a smile and do your best to walk in there radiating control and calmness.

The girls are going back and forth with each other because Lily accidentally splashed some water on Daisy while she was brushing her teeth, and that rattled Daisy. Daisy demands an apology, fully aware Lily splashed her by accident. Lily is unfazed by her sister's attempt to intimidate her, continuing to brush her teeth, mumbling that she's sorry. Lily has grown accustomed to this behaviour from her older sister. Daisy is losing her bananas over Lily's unbothered attitude. In fact, once Lily is done brushing, she turns to you and asks,

"Can you give me a quick shower, mummy?" You respond to Lily, staying quiet about Daisy for now, you want to watch how it unfolds before chiming in, and luckily, Daisy doesn't challenge Lily any further. You let out a quiet breath you didn't realise you were holding.

'This is a win.'

You stayed calm, and the situation defused itself. No further action required.

On a weekday, time flies quickly in the morning. Everybody knows what they're supposed to do, at what time they're supposed to do it. And yet, you keep having to remind everybody to do what they're supposed to do, when they're supposed to do it!

"Get your socks on... Pull your tights up... Where's the hairbrush... Please sit down, let me do your hair... Have you written your gratitude list yet? Did you moisturise your face? Please button your top."

It's the same talk each morning, but you don't mind, that's what you're here for as a mum, right? They're kids, after all, and they'll learn over time — at least they're actually listening to you.

'That's a win.'

One head done. One more to go.

"Daisy, stay still," you say.

"Ow!" Daisy exclaims. "Stop!" she shouts.

"I'm sorry, my love. I'm almost done now," you reply, whilst searching the counter for the leave-in conditioner. "Where did the hairbrush go? Oh, please, please, please put that book back where you found it, Daisy. It's very important for work."

"Oh my gosh, I'm just looking at it. Stop stressing. You're so annoying," Daisy whines.

Your jaw tightens ever so slightly, tension creeping up your shoulders. You take a deep breath. In this moment, you become aware of the choice before you — react in anger

or choose a calm response.

You quickly remind Daisy that the last time she held one of your notebooks, she scribbled all over it, making your notes unreadable. You ask her to put it back on the desk. Mind you, the desk is right in front of her as she is standing while you're finishing her hairstyle. But even with the desk directly in front of her, you watch her extend her right hand to the side and hear the book hit the floor.

'Oh no, she didn't.'

You clench your jaw to avoid blurting out anything crazy, and you take a quiet, slow, deep breath to reset, recognising the tightness in your chest as a signal. You pause to redirect that energy. You then ask her to pick up the book.

The tension rises, and her attitude just entered the room. She picks up the book aggressively and slams it onto the desk.

"Daisy, let's stay calm together. Thank you for following my instructions. Next time, please place it on the desk nicely."

"Ugh. Just stop talking to me. Finish my hair already!"

Your jaw tightens once again.

"Daisy, honey, please be respectful. Otherwise, you'll have to finish your hair yourself."

"No, I won't. You wouldn't let me go out without styling my hair. Just finish already." Daisy smirks.

You're taken aback by her rudeness. Your jaw tightens further, but your face gives nothing away. "I've already moisturised and sectioned your hair for two even buns. Please finish your hairstyle. I warned you not to disrespect me again, and you chose to continue."

You brace yourself because you know exactly what's to come — tantrum incoming. Within a split second, it's all there — crying, screaming, stomping. The whole show.

"But please, Mummy, please finish my hair, please!" she

pleads.

You stick to your word, knowing this is how she learns. A part of you wants to just finish her hair and get on with it. It would save you time and energy for the day ahead.

With all the crying, doubt creeps in.

'Am I being too harsh on her? Oh no — this is going to be another thing that damages her childhood.'

You stop the thought as quickly as it started. It doesn't serve you right now. You must follow through. Gently but firmly, you repeat that she'll have to finish styling her own hair today, reassuring her that most of it is already done.

You head downstairs to finish any last-minute tasks.

Meanwhile, you have a very loud eight-year-old tailing behind you, shouting — no, screaming — hurtful, heart-throbbing words at you. She's saying things you know she'll regret later. According to her — you're apparently a bad mum — the worst out there. All you ever do is try to find ways to annoy her every second of the day. This is not the first time she's said these words to you. And yet they always hurt just the same. You wonder how such words are coming out of this sweet girl you love so deeply.

'How did we even get to this point?' Part of you tries to remind yourself that this is just

another phase. Another part whispers doubt. You do your best to look unfazed by her words. Even as these conflicting thoughts echo in your mind — you start to wonder.

'Where did I go wrong?

Was it because I didn't give her enough eye contact when she was a baby? Did that damage our bond?

Or could it be because I went back to work too early?

No — it must be because I cried so much when I was pregnant

with her.

Like... what is it?

Why is it that when it's great, it's absolutely amazing, but when it's not, it hits somewhere raw.'

At the beginning of this phase, it was bearable. You weren't familiar with it at first, so it came as a shock. You thought it was a phase that would pass. But it just kept getting worse.

'How did we get to this point? Why can't she see how hard I'm trying?'

You finish sorting the lunch bags and go down to Daisy's level, reminding her she has ten minutes to finish up and get out the door. You've never been late before — in fact, Daisy hates being late to anything. She comes to terms with it and runs upstairs to finish her hair.

'I was making such good time today. I woke up early, then Daisy had to take up all of my attention once again. I didn't even get a chance to talk to Lily properly this morning. I don't even have time to feed baby Jake and get him ready for the school run. I'll fix him up a bottle and leave him with John for a feed while I get the girls to school. It shouldn't be a problem. I'll be back before John has to start getting ready for work.'

You're aware that this whole situation has annoyed you quite a bit — it feels as though Daisy enjoys pushing your buttons. She enjoys prodding until she finds the right one to elicit a reaction from you. But the joke's on her now — you destroyed that button. The new you is calm and collected at all times.

In a last attempt to get a reaction from you, Daisy intentionally barges into Lily as she stands near the door putting her coat on. Lily falls to the floor.

Your heart drops. Your reflexes plunge towards Lily as she almost hits the corner of the shoe bench.

As this happens, you hold your breath for two reasons: one, because you're anticipating the pain Lily would feel if she hit the corner. Two, because you don't want to explode and shout at Daisy for pushing her little sister.

Luckily, it was a near miss. Apart from landing on her bottom, she was okay. The shock alone triggers a high-pitched cry — more from surprise than pain.

You're speechless for a moment. You don't understand why there's so much friction in your home.

'What am I getting wrong?'

Lily has her moments too, to be honest. But one thing she does have is resilience. These daily ups and downs are all she's ever known. It makes you wonder how she truly views her sister. She tells you how much she loves Daisy, how she wants to be just like her.

You understand what she means — because you're in awe of Daisy too. When Daisy is relaxed and herself, she's the coolest kid in town, honestly. But you can't help but wonder if, when Lily says she wants to be just like Daisy, that includes the outbursts and disrespect too.

That worries you a lot.

'Is she going to copy all of Daisy's behaviours — the good and the not so good?'

Anxiety kicks in.

You turn to an angry-faced Daisy, her two buns uneven but still presentable, and remind her that we treat each other with kindness.

In your last attempt to brighten the energy before heading out, you smile and sing out, "Positive 100, ladies."

Then you're off for the eight-minute walk, which feels like a 20-minute walk today — thanks to the silence.

You arrive at the school gates on time. The familiar goodbye routine follows — regardless of the fallout. You reconcile with a hug and a quiet, "I love you."

You wave goodbye to both girls and feel a sense of relief. You've done it. You've made it through the morning.

'That's a win.'

In Between

Then, before you know it, you're back on the school grounds.

It's 3:19 p.m. You've put the morning ordeal behind you. You look to the rest of the day with a glimmer of hope, thinking it's less than five hours until bedtime. Just the last stretch to go.

Lily's classroom door opens first, and she runs up to you with a huge grin on her face, her hands raised as she holds out an A4-sized certificate.

"Mummy, look!" she says excitedly.

You give her a huge hug whilst congratulating her on her pupil of the

day certificate.

As you both walk up to Daisy's classroom door, you slip the certificate into Lily's bag.

Daisy's classroom door is already open. Her teacher calls out her name, and here she comes — running straight to you, a huge smile on her face. She knocks you back slightly as she throws her arms around you.

You exchange warm hellos.

You watch as the girls turn to one another, arms wide, grinning as they squeeze tightly. You can tell how much they missed each other. They hardly see each other at school — Lily is in infants, while Daisy is in juniors.

'Now these are the moments I live for, right here. Why can't it always be like this? Is it really too much to ask for?'

As you're walking back from school, there's a corner shop along the way. Sometimes you nip inside to grab snacks — this usually happens on a Friday, movie night. That doesn't stop Daisy from asking almost every day, though.

'You've got to love her persistence, right?'

Well, today is Monday, and you've just done the weekly shop, so there are plenty of snacks at home.

"Mummy, can we please get a snack from the shop?" Daisy asks, her puppy-dog eyes on display.

You reply calmly, explaining that there are plenty of snacks at home after the weekly shop. You mention you can visit the shop another day, choosing your words carefully and avoiding no altogether.

Not that no is a bad word in your household. In fact, you don't shy away from it. It's encouraged when establishing boundaries and protecting yourself. However, more recently, you've come to understand that in moments like this, no has become a trigger for Daisy — something she experiences as control, as a loss of power.

She's trying something new — blackmail.

You're caught off guard by the threat. You start overthinking your actions.

'Where on earth is she learning this? Is it school? Could it be her best friend, Zoe? Is this how it's going to be from now on? No one really talks about these everyday parenting battles.'

You steer the conversation elsewhere.

"So today was PE day, right? What did you do?"

It works. She's walking a little ahead of you now, but at least she's not sulking.

The tension is still there. The old you would have started thinking about how ungrateful Daisy is — but what good would that do? It would only prime your mind for failure in these last few hours.

'How did I actually get here?'

You know you've always wanted to be a mum. Not just to raise children, but to do it with intention.

I know that feeling too.

Ever since I can remember, being a mother has always been a dream of mine.

At the time, other girls would say they wanted to be teachers or architects. When I was asked what I wanted to be when I grew up, I already knew — even at 11. I just wanted to be a mum and a wife, and that wasn't seen as ambitious enough in Western society.

So instead, I'd say I wanted to be an engineer. It felt more socially acceptable.

Nothing could have prepared me for the road of motherhood. It's filled with so many ups. When things are good — when things are going well — I feel completely in my element. And even when they aren't, I've found my way through as best I could. For a long time, that felt good enough.

I'd read my fair share of parenting books and absorbed plenty of advice online. I was doing fine.

However, I'm not sure exactly when the shift happened. Was it the pressure of trying to build more flexibility for my growing family? Was it adding more children into the mix? I'd read that siblings close in age can clash more often — and sometimes it felt painfully accurate.

I don't know when it changed — but it did. And somewhere along the way, parenting started to feel like a tug of war.

'Could it just be that Daisy is growing and becoming her own person?

But that can't be right — can it?'

'Take Olivia, for example. My next-door neighbour has two girls just shy of 11 and 9. She always looks so put together. Her girls are always polite. She's always smiling as we cross paths.'

'What's her secret?'

You're pulled back to the present as your key turns in the front door.

When the Day Slows

On school nights, your evening routine is simple. Once the girls are home, the tablets come off downtime from 3:30 p.m. to 4:30 p.m. They're out, and it's all fun and games for the next hour.

You hand over some nibbles. A quick thanks are exchanged, and they drift back to their screens.

You were once reluctant about screen time — but now you use that hour to get dinner started and feed baby Jake.

A familiar squabble breaks out as both girls keep glancing at each other's screens. Lily shifts her tablet just out of Daisy's view — enough to rattle her into dobbing. That sparks a quick back-and-forth, each of them telling on the other, and the whole thing snowballs into petty chaos.

You glance over with a neutral expression but stay quiet. You breathe slowly and deeply, choosing not to engage, waiting for the storm to pass.

'I won't be dragged into this one,' you tell yourself. Silence is the key — so silence it will be. You've learned to pick your battles carefully, and this is not one of them. No, sir.

The tension eases about seven minutes before the tablets go back on downtime. Daisy realises that every moment spent arguing is eating into her screen time, so she drops it and sinks back into the last few minutes of her favourite game.

It's now 5:30 p.m. The girls have had a quick bath and are now downstairs, ready for dinner.

Lily pipes up, asking if she can watch some TV for a little while. You don't see an issue with it.

She wants to watch Unicorn Academy. Daisy, of course, wants Mr. Bean. They've got about thirty minutes before dinner, but one full episode would use up the entire window — and that's when the political side of you kicks in.

Staying calm and collected, you pick up your phone and explain that you're setting a fifteen-minute timer. Unicorn Academy first. When the timer rings, you'll switch straight to Mr. Bean.

Both girls agree. You breathe out quietly, relieved that you diffused that one before it turned into anything bigger. You catch yourself smiling — amused at how good you've become at spotting problems before they even start.

You like to think of yourself as a problem preventer rather than a problem solver.

'I mean, who actually enjoys solving problems anyway?'

It's 6:12 p.m., and dinner's on the table.

Both timers have rung.

However, the TV is still on.

This routine barely changes. You'd think everyone would know what to do — and when to do it.

You call everyone over to the table.

"But Mum, I'm not hungry," Daisy moans.

"Yeah, me too," Lily agrees.

"I want to watch TV," Daisy adds.

"Yeah, me too," Lily follows.

You pause, taken aback. You'd agreed the TV would go off once time was up — and a moment ago, everyone seemed on the same page.

You glance at Lily and notice it: the way she's watching Daisy, quietly taking notes on how to respond.

Not only is Daisy being difficult — she's teaching her little sister to do the same.

And then you hear your sweet Daisy's voice say to Lily,

"Mum is so annoying. She's always bossing us around. Let's just not listen to her."

You clench your jaw — tighter than you did this morning.

'It's one thing for Daisy to be disrespectful.

It's a whole other thing when she starts influencing her little sister too.

Will she recruit Jake next?'

Your thoughts spiral — and before you can stop yourself, the words come out.

"Daisy."

"Please do not influence your sister this way. We show kindness and respect in this house."

Daisy looks straight at you, her face tightening.

She huffs, then drags herself over to the table.

Lily trails after her.

You sit beside Lily as Jake settles into his high chair.

Everyone is seated now.

You look around the table at your babies and offer a small, steady smile — hoping it helps shift the energy.

Spaghetti bolognese — a family favourite.

You decided to keep things simple tonight after the shaky morning. There was no way you were tackling broccoli and peas.

You know the girls are hungry — they've been asking when dinner would be ready since 5:30.

But as she sits down, you glance at Daisy and catch the look on her face — tight, unimpressed.

Clearly, someone's not happy with the chef's special tonight.

"Mum," Daisy snaps. "I didn't want spaghetti bolognese."

You take a slow breath, genuinely confused. You're certain spag bol is her favourite.

"Look — I even added extra cheese. You love mozzarella," you say, trying to keep things light.

"I don't want it," Daisy says flatly. "I want something else."

You pause.

'Never, in her eight years, have I made her something else when she's refused what's already on the table.

I mean, yes — sometimes I ask for suggestions beforehand. Sometimes I offer options.

So why does she feel the need to challenge me for the eleventh consecutive day?

As if I'm suddenly going to say, yes, what would you like instead, darling?'

You glance over at Lily. She's still eating, quiet and focused, but you notice the slight tilt of her head at Daisy's refusal.

Your stomach tightens.

You worry that Daisy's defiance isn't just noise anymore — that Lily might be taking notes, thinking this is how you behave.

A spike of panic hits.

'Why does it have to be so difficult to put food — food you know you love — into your mouth? Simple.'

You keep your voice steady as you repeat that spaghetti bolognese — with extra cheese — is her favourite.

You pull a careful smile, trying to make it reach your eyes.

Then you make one last attempt — pulling Daisy's favourite silly face, the one that usually breaks the tension.

It doesn't work.

You watch Daisy's plate inch closer to the edge of the table.

Slow. Deliberate.

The scrape of ceramic stops — then the sound hits.

Splat.

Your chest tightens.

You freeze.

This has never happened before.

'I must be seeing things.

Did she really just push her plate off the table?'

You lock eyes with Daisy.

She doesn't flinch.

There's a small, knowing smile on her face — the kind that quietly asks, what are you going to do about it?

Everything happens at once.

Before you can gather your thoughts, you snap.

You absolutely lose it.

You don't register the words coming out of your mouth — only the volume.

The force.

All the tension from this morning, the days leading up to now, erupts all at once.

When it's over, Daisy is bawling her eyes out.

Her face, crumpled.

Tears, streaming.

Her breath, hitching as she stares at you like you're the worst person in the world.

'Ugh.'

All of the day's progress is in the bin.

That familiar mum guilt creeps in.

'How does a person who isn't even half my age get this reaction out of me?'

Lily is reading the room, instinctively taking a backseat this time.

She's gotten very good at sensing when the air shifts.

She must be thinking, mum's gone mad.

Daisy is screaming at you now — and you know you'd be the biggest hypocrite alive if you told her to stop.

You know saying anything else right now will only make it worse.

So you stay silent.

Daisy is trying to get a reaction from you — but you don't give her one.

You've learned the hard way that engaging right now only fuels another argument.

'It's better I stay quiet.'

You hate this — the silence.

You've always told yourself you wouldn't be the kind of parent who uses it.

Over the years, you've taken pride in being the kind of parent who talks things through from the very start.

You'd name the big emotion Daisy was feeling, helping her identify it instead of being consumed by it.

You'd explain what had happened, how it led here, and then offer options to move forward.

Over the years, this approach worked — or so you thought.

It didn't always bring instant calm or perfect resolutions, but it meant Daisy knew you were there.

That you weren't going anywhere.

That she was loved, even in the peak of a tantrum.

Or so you thought.

Now, trying to talk it out only makes things worse.

She tells you you're only trying to make her angry — that

you're doing it on purpose.

'Is it because she's eight now?

Does she just hate my voice?'

You never know what to do.

You can hear her yelling at you to answer — but the moment you do, she tells you to stop talking.

You can't win.

Silence carries you through the rest of dinner.

She ends up fixing herself another plate — and to no surprise, she eats it all.

You're already thinking about the battle of bedtime — the never-ending series that airs every evening between 7:00 p.m. and 8:30 p.m.

Around three months ago, you changed the bedtime routine by moving bath time to before dinner.

It's made evenings flow a little better. After eating, all that's left is brushing teeth and getting into bed.

You feel quietly chuffed with yourself for thinking it through — as if you're up for a medal.

It's funny how the smallest changes can make you feel like you're winning as a mum.

Everyone is in their pyjamas and getting into bed.

You're absolutely exhausted at this point.

You consider making a small cup of coffee to get through the bedtime story, but that would mean dragging yourself downstairs all over again.

A flicker of guilt rises from your outburst with Daisy earlier — followed closely by embarrassment.

Your mind drifts to stuffing your face with chocolate while binge-watching Bridgerton on Netflix. That would make you feel better, at least for a little while.

Then you remember the optimistic woman you were this morning — the one who thought today would be different.

The best thing now is getting the kids to bed — and yourself too.

It's still only Monday, after all.

You pick the smallest bedtime story possible and whisk through it at speed.

Your patience is paper-thin. All you want to do is walk out and shut the bedroom door while they bombard you with a dozen last-minute philosophical questions — a final attempt to stay awake for as long as possible.

Since yawns are contagious, you try fake-yawning in the hope it rubs off.

Then you lower your voice and keep your answers short.

Lily starts snoring within minutes.

Daisy follows soon after.

'Success.'

You drag your feet out of their room and into yours, baby Jake still in your arms.

Your shift is almost done now.

Baby Jake is dozing off as he finishes his milk.

You stare at him in quiet awe, remembering when Daisy was that small too.

'How time flies.'

It's 9:28 p.m., and you're clocking out now.

'What a day.

Let's do it all again tomorrow — minus the outburst.'

'Goodnight, me.'

Sleep tight.

II

Part Two | How It Lives With You

Part One helped you see yourself more clearly — not as a problem to fix, but as a woman navigating real, layered moments.
Part Two is about shifting how you respond to those moments, so your actions begin to reflect the awareness you already have.

A Shift In Focus

This book isn't about overloading you with theory or academic breakdowns of parenting.

It's a guide designed to help you shift how you show up in the moments that already make up your day.

You already know more than you think — this part is about creating the space to act from that place.

This part is here to support you in showing up with clarity and intention — so the energy you bring into your home reflects the values you already carry within you.

I know you don't have endless hours. You're in the thick of parenting — juggling, managing, and sometimes surviving. So this book isn't about taking notes for later.

It's about three shifts you can begin applying immediately — today. These three shifts invite you to move differently, to embody a new way of showing up.

As you do, you'll notice a transformation in your approach to parenting.

What I share here is shaped by lived experience — my own, and what I've consistently seen resonate with other parents navigating similar moments.

If you're a parent who can hold deep love and deep frustration in the same breath — this part is for you. The same child you adore can also be the one who pushes you right to the edge. That tension is real, and it doesn't mean you're doing anything wrong.

When you look around and see other parents who seem to have it all together, you might wonder how they're doing it so well. The truth is, some may be managing — but most are figuring it out as they go, just like you. They're just not airing out their hardest moments in public. And let's be honest — neither are you.

People say parenting isn't easy — but they rarely explain what's hard. You love your child, want the best for them, and would do anything for their happiness — yet they can test your patience like nothing else. At times, you question yourself, feeling the nurturing part of you begin to slip away.

Then there are the beautiful moments — the ones that fill your heart so completely that when you count your blessings, you count that same child twice. Parenting is both chaos and beauty. Love and learning, all at once.

Lasting change doesn't begin with what you do — it begins with how you think.

Actions matter, of course. But when change is driven by action alone, it rarely lasts. Without a shift in mindset, old patterns quietly return.

This is your invitation to step out of the endless cycle of doing more, fixing more, trying harder — and instead focus on how you think, what you tell yourself, and how you see your role as a parent.

Because that's where true change begins.

As you read Part One, you may have noticed just how busy the mother's mind was at any given moment. Worry. Guilt. Second-guessing. A constant stream of thoughts questioning every reaction and decision. That inner dialogue wasn't background noise — it was shaping everything that followed.

And this is where your shift begins.

The path to harmony in your home doesn't start with changing your child — it starts with changing your inner landscape.

Not their mind. Yours.

With that foundation in place, it's time to shift your focus.

The next three shifts are here to gently realign your mindset — one layer at a time — so peace, confidence, and connection can begin to flow naturally.

A Quick Note

This book is intended for informational and educational purposes only. It reflects personal insight and lived experience, not professional advice.

As a parent, you know your child and family best. Every situation is unique, and this content is not a substitute for guidance from qualified professionals when individualised support is needed. Always trust your judgment and seek appropriate advice for your specific circumstances.

SHIFT 1 | Releasing Mum Guilt

You don't need to shame yourself for being human. All that mum guilt you're carrying isn't helping you move forward or parent the way you truly want.

For years, I'd heard about mum guilt. On a surface level, I thought I understood it. But it wasn't until I sat with my thoughts one day — after a huge disagreement with my oldest — that I realised just how much guilt I'd been holding onto. For every fallout we had, whether big or small, I added it to my "Mum Guilt Bag".

For every time I lost my cool, I added that to the bag too.

For every moment she accused me of not loving her because I'd shouted, I added that in as well.

I've carried this invisible bag since pregnancy, and with each child, it only got heavier — turning into a suitcase with broken wheels that I was dragging behind me. It shaped how I saw the world, the choices I made, and even the challenges I was willing to face. It controlled me — and I didn't notice how heavy it had become.

It wasn't until I felt the strain that I finally stopped to look at what I'd been carrying. That's when I realised I needed to sort through it and move forward — easing the anxiety I carried about my future relationships with my children.

When I understood that the future is shaped by what I do today, I found the clarity and confidence to finally address the guilt that had been building for years.

Today, I can change my mindset — and that shift will transform my actions. By doing so, I'm intentionally shaping my future outcomes and becoming a better version of myself than yesterday.

I don't need to be perfect. I just need to be better than I was yesterday. That simple truth took away a great deal of pressure.

Give yourself that same grace. Not as a phrase you repeat, but as something you actually allow.

Let go of the guilt you're carrying from today — and from all the days that came before it.

You're already doing meaningful work as a parent. You wouldn't be here — or reading this — if you weren't. Why else would you dedicate your precious time and energy to transforming your mindset around parenting, if not out of love and intention?

This book didn't just stumble into your hands — you aligned yourself to receive it.

How to Interrupt the Guilt Cycle

Start by creating a list of moments where you've felt mum guilt. To help you begin, think in gentle time frames rather than trying to remember everything at once. You might start with moments from this week, then earlier this year, and then earlier seasons of your parenting. Let your mind move naturally.

Dedicate at least 15 minutes to this practice. Find a quiet space, and don't worry about writing it neatly or saying it the "right" way. Write it raw. This isn't about sounding articulate — it's about being honest.

If writing feels restrictive, you can speak your thoughts aloud into your phone and let them turn into text instead.

Whether your list ends up being one item or pages full, that's okay. The goal isn't quantity. The goal is to come face to face with what you've been carrying — to humanise the guilt so it no longer sits unexamined in the background of your mind.

Once you've written it all down, read through each item slowly. For every statement rooted in guilt, ask yourself how it can be reframed — shifting it from guilt to growth. What did this moment teach you? What does it reveal about your values, your care, or your capacity to reflect?

This is where release begins — not by erasing the past, but by changing the meaning you've been attaching to it.

Example:
Mum Guilt:
I often feel guilty about cutting conversations short with Daisy most nights, even though I know she's trying to stay up longer. I also know she's just trying to connect with me, but I'm usually so tired and impatient. I hate that I dismiss her attempts to talk.
Statement:
In the past, *I carried guilt for cutting conversations short with Daisy most nights.*

__Now,__ I've created a two question token system. Once she's in bed, we spend up to ten minutes talking through her questions or topics of choice. This allows me to set clear expectations around bedtime while still making space for connection and meaningful conversation.

Get creative with this process and make it fun. You never know what new little traditions might grow from it.

Once you're done writing your list, you can either keep it or tear it up — both are valid releases, and you should follow what feels right for you.

Mum guilt isn't a one-time experience. When it shows up again, return to this process and meet it with the same awareness.

SHIFT 2 | Releasing the Illusion of Control

Let go of the control you never had.

Many of us don't realise how deeply the need to control has been woven into our experience of motherhood — not because we're doing something wrong, but because of what's been placed on us.

Your role was never to fix life — or your child — but to show up with awareness, steadiness, and presence. You were never meant to control what's unfolding around you.

Motherhood shifts quietly, often without you realising it's happening. From the moment you become pregnant, you're flooded with information — what you can and can't eat, how you should sleep, which products to avoid, what to monitor, what to prepare for.

It's an overload of guidance, rules, and opinions — and you're left to navigate it all while being told it's "for the best."

At that stage, it *feels* like control. You make choices, follow guidelines, and manage what happens to your body.

And then labour arrives — and control dissolves. You can prepare and plan as much as you want, but you can't control what happens in that moment. And yet, as soon as the baby arrives, you return to what's familiar — managing everything.

Pay attention to the word *manage*.

Because from the very beginning, that's what we tell ourselves. When you first look down at your tiny, helpless baby, instinct takes over — and with it, the urge to manage every detail. And if you're not aware of this pattern — most of us aren't — don't beat yourself up about it. Every mother recognises the beautiful chaos that unfolds once a baby enters your world.

We create the illusion that we're managing it all — but in reality, the baby sets the rhythm. Feeding times, sleep patterns, the in-betweens — they lead, and we adapt. Still, our natural instinct tries to bring order. So we plan bath time to encourage sleep, choose feeding routines that feel supportive, and build structures to help everyone feel secure.

This version of control — disguised as "management" — quietly becomes the norm.

And it's not wrong — it's deeply human. The problem begins when that instinct doesn't evolve. We don't stop at bath time or feeding schedules — we continue to manage as they grow. Before we realise it, we're managing an eight-year-old the same way we once managed a baby — just with more complex tools.

But here's the good — and even better — news:

You are only in control of yourself.

And, you never really had control over anyone else in the first place.

Let yourself sit with that.

For years, I tried to hold everything together. My heart was always in the right place. I believed that if I created strong, simple routines, my children would feel secure — and everything would flow.

Especially during those early toddler years — when emotions ran high and meltdowns felt constant — I felt responsible for how they felt. I believed that if I managed situations better, they would be calm and happy.

If meals were on time, transitions smoother, or plans better thought through, I told myself the tantrums could be avoided.

Eventually, I realised my role was to guide, not to control or manage.

I had been mistaking responsibility for control.

And the moment that truth landed, the weight I'd been carrying for years began to lift.

When I began living from the truth that I was only in control of myself, everything softened. I parented with more calm, more confidence. I took responsibility for my thoughts, my words, my actions — and in doing so, I modelled accountability for my children.

Letting go of control allows me to rebuild the bond I want with my children — slowly, honestly, and with intention. It reminds me that while some patterns take time to heal, they are not permanent. Trust, connection, and communication can be restored — one consistent moment at a time.

When you live from the understanding that you are only in control of yourself, something subtle but powerful changes. When your child expresses anger or frustration, you no longer rush to control the moment. You stay with yourself — and respond from there.

And that quiet strength becomes their greatest teacher.

This work asks for trust. For intention. For honesty with yourself. And above all, awareness — of how you show up, moment by moment.

How to Lead Without Control

I began releasing the illusion of control through reminders that grounded me back to myself.

I would return to one steady truth: *I am in control of myself.*

I wrote these reminders on Post-it notes and placed them around the house. Each one became a quiet cue — a pause. A moment to breathe out twice and reset, gently reinforcing the message without force.

At first, these reminders were only meant for me — a way to build awareness without effort. But over time, my children began noticing them too.

What started as a personal practice became a quiet movement within our home.

It didn't make our home peaceful 24/7 — we're human, after all — but it did create a shift. And i began to notice a growing sense of ownership in all of us.

Let this practice be rooted in your growth — not in a desire to change your child. Live this mindset openly, not to provoke different behaviour, but because you've chosen to grow.

Imagine your child learning — through your example — that emotions don't need fixing, just space. That kind of safety changes everything.

Being in control of yourself doesn't mean you'll never slip up. You're human. What changes is what happens next. Because when you do falter, you can take accountability without shifting blame or carrying guilt.

That's growth.

That's transformation.

Choose a reminder that fits naturally into your life.

It might be a Post-it note placed where you'll see it often. It might be your phone wallpaper — something visual that anchors you each time you pick it up. Or it could be the message on your morning alarm, gently setting the tone before the day begins.

These aren't prompts to control yourself — they're cues to return to awareness.

The more aware you become of where control truly lives, the lighter parenting begins to feel.

SHIFT 3 | Live Positive 100

Positive 100 isn't about doing more. It's about how you meet the moments you're already in.

Once guilt loosens and control softens, something else becomes possible. You get to choose how you show up—moment by moment.

In my household, we call this "Positive 100."

It's not a technique—it's an approach to everyday life.

It's an approach your whole family can use—toddlers, school-aged kids, and you. And the reason it works is simple: what's repeated becomes familiar.

Positive 100 is built on something you already recognise. It's the moment you choose perspective over reaction. It's looking for what *can* be done instead of staying stuck on what went wrong. It's helping your child shift their thinking when emotions are high, without dismissing how they feel. It's acknowledging the silver lining without pretending the hard part didn't exist.

This way of thinking already lives within you. Giving it a name—and treating it like a shared value—changed how it showed up in my home. Positive 100 became a simple anchor we could return to, again and again, to reinforce a growth mindset in everyday moments

To support how we show up day to day, I shaped Positive 100 into a simple framework — an acronym we could return to when emotions run high or clarity felt lost. Not as a set of rules—but as a shared reference point for how we wanted our home to feel.

The idea was never to control behaviour. It was to give us a common language—something steady we could come back to in moments that felt messy, rushed, or emotionally charged.

Each letter in Positive 100 reflects a value we aim to practise, both at home and within ourselves. They're not ideals to perfect, but reminders to return to—much like values you might see guiding a workplace culture or a school ethos, yet rarely written down within families.

This framework became a quiet anchor for us. A way to stay aligned without constant correction, and to reinforce the kind of growth mindset we wanted to model consistently.

You're free to take this as it is, or let it evolve naturally to reflect what matters most in your own home. What's important isn't the wording—it's having something shared, recognisable, and easy to return to when perspective is needed.

For us, Positive 100 is shaped around the following values:

- **P – Patience**
- **O – Optimism**
- **S – Support**
- **I – Intention**
- **T – Trust**
- **I – Integrity**
- **V – Vulnerability**
- **E – Empathy**

Together, they form a reference point—not for perfection, but for awareness.

And once that awareness exists, living Positive 100 becomes less about effort, and more about practice.

How to Live Positive 100 Daily

Here's how Positive 100 took shape in our home—across different ages, moods, and emotional moments.

It sounded something like this:

"In our home, everyone is allowed to feel their emotions fully and honestly. Positive 100 doesn't mean pretending you're okay when you're not. It means you're encouraged to feel what you feel—and then choose how you move forward with awareness."

That distinction matters.

Positive 100 creates space for emotions without letting them run the show.

It teaches that feelings are valid, but reactions are a choice.

For example, if one of my children becomes upset because I refuse to do their hair after they've been disrespectful, they're absolutely allowed to feel angry or disappointed.

What Positive 100 changes is how we *frame* the moment.

Usually, a child might think:

"I'm really angry that Mum won't do my hair. She refuses. She doesn't care. I don't like her right now."

Through the Positive 100 approach, that same moment is reframed:

"I'm really angry that Mum won't do my hair, **and** I still love her. I shouldn't have spoken to her that way when she warned me. Now I have to do it myself, but at least she already sectioned and moisturised it for me. Next time, I'll try to respond better — she was only trying to help."

Notice the language here. We replace 'but' with 'and'.

'But' creates opposition — it teaches a child that one feeling cancels out another. 'And' allows two truths to exist at the same time.

Positive 100 teaches your child that they can feel angry and still feel loved. They can feel disappointed and still stay connected. They can make a mistake and still learn from it.

This "and" way of thinking didn't come from correction.

It came from modelling.

When my children are around, I practice Positive 100 out loud in real moments — especially when I'm working through my own challenges or heightened emotions. I intentionally narrate my thoughts and feelings, not to lecture, but to demonstrate how perspective works in real time.

This is where your influence as a parent lives.

When children hear you name frustration, accountability, and perspective clearly, they learn how to do the same internally.

Over time, and with repetition, they begin to adopt a growth mindset naturally—not because they were told to, but because they saw it lived.

Positive 100 becomes less about words, and more about how your home *responds* to challenges.

Once Positive 100 found its place in our home, it naturally started showing up everywhere.

I'd say it at random moments throughout the day — walking past the kids' rooms, while cooking, on the school run, or right in the middle of a good laugh. Sometimes I'd sing it, sometimes I'd dance it, sometimes I'd say it just being my goofy self.

What I noticed was this: when positivity becomes part of your everyday household culture, the energy shifts without effort.

Before long, Positive 100 stopped feeling like a phrase and started living as a mindset. It echoed through our home — woven into how we spoke, how we repaired, how we forgave, and how we reconnected. The atmosphere softened. Grace came more easily. Harmony stopped feeling like something we had to force.

And there you have it — three intentional shifts designed to bring you back to yourself as a parent.

At the heart of each shift is the same truth: everything begins with mindset. When the way you think softens and expands, the way you respond naturally follows.

These pages were never about teaching you how to parent. They were about offering perspective — creating space for you to notice what you already know, and giving language to instincts you've been carrying all along.

When you focus on what's within your control — your thoughts, your reactions, your presence — you create a ripple effect. Calm replaces tension. Accountability replaces guilt. Connection replaces control.

As you move forward, allow awareness to guide you. Let it meet you on the heavy days and steady you on the lighter ones. Parenting isn't about getting it right — it's about staying present. And with a grounded mindset, presence becomes the foundation everything else grows from.

Conclusion

Before you close this book, I want to pause with you for a moment.

Take a deep breath — really, do it — and recognise how far you've already come.

You've taken the time to sit, read, reflect, and invest in your growth as a parent. That's not something small. And it's not something everyone chooses to do. It takes courage to look inward — to question old patterns, to loosen guilt, to release control, and to begin showing up differently, even when it feels uncomfortable.

That courage deserves to be seen.

As you move forward, remember this: there will still be messy moments. There will still be days that feel long, loud, and full of emotion — yours and your child's. But those moments no longer define you. Because now, you carry awareness. You understand that real change begins in the mind — not in the noise around you, but in the steadiness you build within yourself.

If it feels supportive, take a moment to acknowledge what you already bring to your parenting. Perhaps it's your patience, your creativity, your ability to listen, or your willingness to try again. Naming these strengths isn't about ego — it's about recognising that you are already capable, already learning, already growing.

You don't need to be a perfect parent to raise children who feel safe, secure, and loved. You only need to be present — open to learning, quick to repair, slow to react, and willing to begin again tomorrow.

That's love in action.

That's growth.

That's grace.

So go forward knowing this: you are already enough. You are already doing an incredible job. And your children are deeply fortunate to have a parent who chooses love, awareness, and intention — every single day.

Acknowledgments

To my husband, thank you for always being my biggest supporter. Your kindness, strength and integrity has been a stable foundation in which I have been able to grow and live my life with purpose, authenticity and love.

To my children and nieces, you are my brightest stars. Thank you for guiding me with your light, to be the best possible version of myself.

To my mum, although I could never repay you for everything you have done for me, I will, however, live my life trying to do so. Thank you for your love, generosity and resilience. You are an extraordinary woman and my role model.

To my mother in law, thank you for raising an incredible son and for accepting me as your own. I am forever grateful for your strength, positivity and support.

To my four sisters, thank you for your friendships, humour and motivation. There is never a dull moment in your company, and I cherish all the memories we share.

About the Author

Amina Suarez is a wife and homeschooling mum who cares deeply about how children experience home. She believes that parenting isn't about getting it right all the time, but about creating an environment where children feel safe, seen, and loved — even on the days that feel heavy or messy.

Her work is shaped by lived experience, reflection, and a commitment to personal growth. Amina writes for mums who want to parent with intention, not perfection, and who understand that the way we show up matters just as much as what we say.

At the heart of everything she shares is a simple belief: when adults do the inner work, children benefit. Through her writing, Amina hopes to offer reassurance, perspective, and practical shifts that help families move with more calm, connection, and clarity.

For More Visit: www.positive100.com

Scan the QR code below to receive your complimentary Parenting Strengths worksheet.
Enter your email and it will be sent directly to you.

Strength grows where attention goes.

www.ingramcontent.com/pod-product-compliance
Lightning Source LLC
Chambersburg PA
CBHW020648160726
47991CB00003B/1083